CW01475705

F E N D E R

Custom Shop

G U I T A R   G A L L E R Y

FENDER

Custom Shop

GUITAR GALLERY

Photography by Pitkin Studio

Text by Richard R. Smith

A Joint Venture Publication of

Fender

HAL•LEONARD

Fender Custom Shop

Published by **HAL LEONARD CORPORATION**

7777 West Bluemound Road

P.O. Box 13819

Milwaukee, Wisconsin 53213

Printed in U.S.A.

ISBN 0-7935-5065-3

ISBN 0-7935-5067-X (collector's edition)

F/N 099-5012-000

F/N 099-5012-100 (collector's edition)

TABLE OF CONTENTS

This book is dedicated to the memory of two good friends, James L. D'Aquisto and Mark D. Wittenberg. Both made immeasurable contributions to Fender and the music industry as a whole. They will be greatly missed, but never forgotten.

Custom Shop

by Richard R. Smith

■ In the field of musical instruments and guitar building, Fender is the world's leader, the product and image that has made the biggest mark on our culture this century. The company's uncomplicated wooden, plastic, and metal powerhouses of sound—which have changed very little technically since the 1950s—still set the standard in an age increasingly dominated by microchips and obscure technologies. Fender guitars embody a particular genius for doing things right in a simple, straight-forward manner. Moreover, like Levi's, Corvettes, and A-2 flight jackets, Fender guitars have come to symbolize youth, freedom, and just plain fun (one reason you can almost always spot one in a beer commercial). Their sounds and shapes permeate our popular culture with visual and sonic images that say, "Yeah, this is cool. This is hip."

■ You don't have to scratch your head and think too hard to remember hearing a Fender; they've been played worldwide since the 1950s. James Burton's solo on Ricky Nelson's "Hello Mary Lou" and Jimmy Page's on Led Zeppelin's "Stairway to Heaven" are just two examples. The Beatles played twin Stratocasters on "Nowhere Man." Jimi Hendrix created his explosive sonic style on a Strat, too. The list of other musicians who played or play Fender instruments reads like a *Who's Who* of the music world. The guitars have been seen

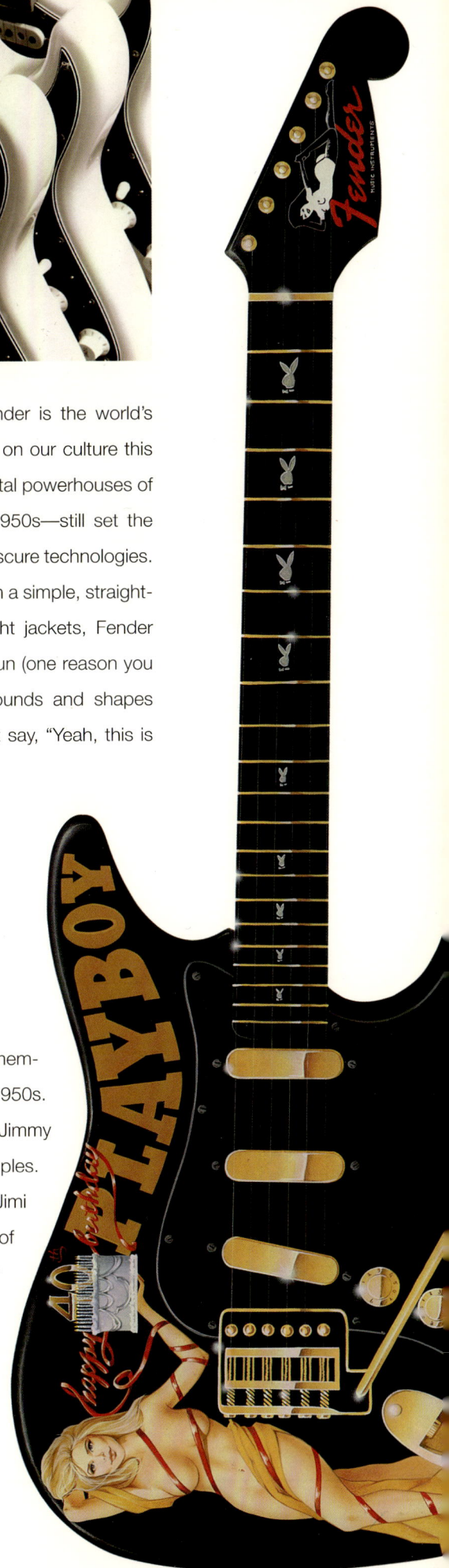

on stage with virtually all the stars: Elvis, the Rolling Stones, Bob Dylan, Bruce Springsteen, Johnny Cash, Jon Bon Jovi, David Bowie, Alabama, Vince Gill, Buck Owens, Bonnie Raitt,…an endless list in all fields of music. Fender guitars have become timeless classics.

■ The subject of this book is the Fender Custom Shop, and more importantly, some of the timeless classics produced at its almost ironically nondescript industrial-park facility in Corona, California (behind what many locals call the "orange curtain," the wall of smog that often separates coastal and inland southern California). It's hard to sum up what this place is, but the Fender company and its employees call it the Dream Factory. One reason why is that a customer can get almost any guitar he wants from the Custom Shop. It produces almost the entire spectrum of guitarlike instruments, from the finest jazz acoustics to a new line called the Relics (solidbody electrics with distressed finishes, intentionally made to look 40 years old). Custom Shop instruments are to guitar playing what finely tuned Ferraris are to car racing. In these guitars, high-quality workmanship and precision engineering combine. With beautiful one-of-a-kind "art guitars," as general manager John Page often refers to them, the Custom Shop takes Fender up another notch, adding a component of world-class hand-crafted artistry.

■ The Custom Shop is the Dream Factory for another reason. The people working there are for the most part doing exactly what they want to do: building guitars for a living, taking personal pride in custom products with countless hours of intensive labor, and working hand in hand with the top guitarists of the world. All of the artists, engineers, and technicians there could find employment elsewhere, many in fields other than guitar building. But as master builder Fred Stuart recently said, "We might find higher pay—certainly the engineers that work here could—but we all love guitars. And besides, it's pretty cool hanging around with James Burton at the trade shows."

BIRTH OF THE CUSTOM SHOP

The idea for today's Custom Shop began in the early 1980s. Fender had several requests from artists for custom guitars, orders filled by the company's R&D model shop. The craftsmen making these guitars, like John Page, envisioned a much larger operation, serving the public as well—something like Martin's custom shop, founded in 1979. But the company was not in a position to pursue the idea at the time. The U.S. guitar market in general was suffering, due to foreign competition and a declining interest in guitars among teenagers, and Fender in particular had lost much of its previous glory. In the midst of these tough times, a custom shop was not a priority, but the seed was planted.

■ CBS, which had owned Fender since 1965, brought in new management in 1981 to turn the company around. Despite their success in doing so, by 1984 CBS decided to get out of the musical instrument business altogether, and in 1985 sold the company to a group of investors led by Fender president William Schultz. The new owners hired George F. Blanda Jr. as a custom builder, but he ended up becoming the senior project engineer for guitar R&D, making prototypes and new designs.

■ Page, who had worked at the company since 1978, quit his job in R&D to pursue a music career in early 1986. He observes, "By Christmas time I had depleted every penny I had ever had." Facing the prospects of poverty, he called his friends at Fender. The timing was perfect, as Fender's Dan Smith was already talking with Michael Stevens, a highly respected Texas-based maker, about a new project—starting what the guys in the old R&D model shop had imagined, a true custom shop. In addition, Michael would be making his own

Stevens line in California for Fender. Dan Smith gave Page an option: work in R&D or with Stevens. Page, who loved building guitars, chose the latter. In early 1987 Stevens was packing up for his move to California, and Page was setting up the Shop.

■ Clearly, at first the Custom Shop was a calculated way for Fender to regain some lost glory. The new owners thought that the Custom Shop would be a prestigious affair—two guys building Rolls Royces in the building out back. The first space was a paltry 850 square feet next to Fender's main factory. (The Custom Shop and Fender's main plant have always operated as separate entities.) As for numbers, the company expected John and Michael to build five or six guitars a month. The two builders expected about the same, until the first guitars went out to rave reviews in June 1987. (Work order #0001 was to refinish a '57 Strat out of stock for Buddy Rogers Music. Order #0006, for guitarist Elliot Easton, called for a left-handed Thinline Telecaster with a Foam Green finish, maple top, alder back, and a bird's-eye maple neck.) In the next three months almost 600 more orders came in.

■ By the end of 1987 the company expanded the operation, which, like the main plant, has continued steady growth ever since. Because of the demand, the Custom Shop became more than just a showcase for Stevens and Page. New master builders gradually came on board, and the Shop started making a significant impact on the whole Fender line, from top to bottom. Page, who had corporate experience, soon became the manager for both the Custom Shop and R&D (he recently dropped his R&D responsibilities). Combining the two at this point was a brilliant stroke for the company. In a guitar maker's version of the trickle-down theory, ideas, features, and production techniques that worked on custom guitars found their way into the lower-priced Fender lines produced in the U.S. and overseas. In that sense each Custom Shop guitar was a guinea pig in a guitar building laboratory. For example, most of the Signature Series guitars, like the Eric Clapton model, started as Custom Shop guitars.

■ The Shop also quickly became a way to solve a problem that had plagued Fender during the CBS era: staying on the cutting edge.

Its builders worked daily with artists, learning their latest needs. Unlike a huge assembly plant, Page's operation adapted to changes and suggestions overnight. Recently Page commented, "We are still supposed to be the guys that are very lean and very quick, right in the marketplace because we're dealing with the customers and dealers every single day, unlike a marketing operation that's dealing on a different level." In 1990 he said, "Trends change, and we want to be able to address them. The Custom Shop is trying to lead the way in getting Fender to make any kind of guitar you would want to get." That includes guitars with very un-Fender features, like set necks.

■ In the guitar industry, certain companies traditionally have been known for certain types of guitars. While Fender always dominated the market for solidbody guitars with bolt-on necks, Gibson dominated the set-neck field. (The Les Paul, for example, has a set neck.) Another way for Fender to grow and to reestablish its image in the 1980s was to knock down old preconceptions and produce credible alternatives to the other companies' guitars. The Custom Shop's first entry into this almost alien world was the Stevens LJ. The set-neck Telecaster was next, followed by the D'Aquisto jazz guitars, introduced in early 1994. (This project was the result of over 10 years of planning by Fender executives. The late Jimmy D'Aquisto—builder of some of the finest guitars of this century—personally trained master builder Stephen Stern.) Page said recently, "When you look at them from a unit point of view or from a dollar point of view, the set-neck guitars like the D'Aquistos are almost background noise level in this company. But if you look at them from a spiritual point of view, they're deafening, because they say so much about what we're trying to do." He added, "We're just trying to make the absolute best guitars we can make, whether it's a bolt-on solidbody or whether it's a jazz guitar, a set-neck, or a semi-acoustic."

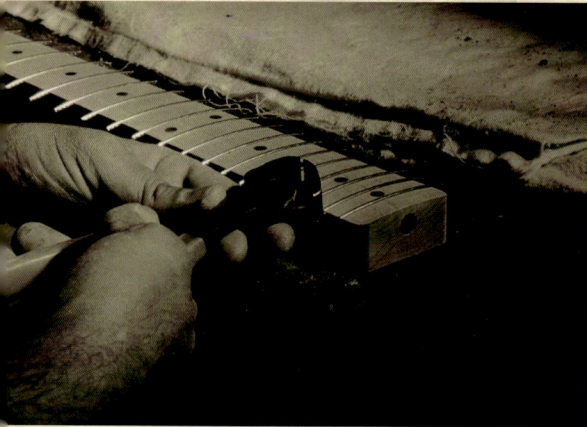

THE CUSTOM SHOP TODAY

The facility, which as of April 1995 measured 18,000 square feet, has become in essence what Page calls a craftsmen's co-op. Individuals and small groups of builders share space and resources, and thus practice their artistry more effectively. The operation has about 50 employees, including builders and apprentices. The master builders are J.W. Black, Mark Kendrick, John English, Fred Stuart, Alan Hamel, Gene Baker, John Suhr, and archtop maker Stern. All bring unique experiences and skills to the task. Page still works on guitars when he can find the time, and Blanda still plays a significant role in the designs. Steve Boulanger adds his expertise in tool design. Each builder has a signature decal to identify his guitars, thus maintaining his own identity while contributing to Fender. When there's an opening for workers at the Custom Shop, Page tries to hire top performers from the main Fender plant. They become apprentices, learning custom building techniques from the master builders.

■ Other artists at the Shop include wood-carver George Amicay, who does detail work featured on guitars like the Phoenix. The creations of Dru WhiteFeather, a Native American craftsman, are showcased in guitars like the White Buffalo Telecaster (embellished with wood, leather, turquoise, and silver). Artist Pamelina Hovnatanian does renderings for most of the special projects, like the Harley-Davidson Strat. Says Page, "She's the first person I've met who can put onto paper what I see in my head."

■ The Custom Shop has always done modifications to existing models and has always built completely custom instruments. "We will build as crazy as people want to pay," said Page in 1990. Michael Stevens, who eventually quit Fender and moved back to Texas, made a solidbody electric banjo complete with pedal steel tuners for one customer. Today the Shop makes production runs of limited edition products too complex for the main factory, like a batch of rosewood Telecasters for a Japanese dealer. At the other end of the spectrum are the very limited number of art guitars, many seen in this book. For customers simply looking to personalize their own instruments, the Shop also produces a line of accessories—pickguards, picks, pickups, straps, gig bags.

■ Although limited compared to the main factory, production at the Custom Shop totals between 12 and 25 instruments a day, and anywhere from 4,000 to 6,000 guitars a year. But it really depends. Page explained in July 1995, "Last month I think we produced 12 guitars a day. A month earlier it was 22…. The most important thing to us is that the guitars are excellent before they go out. Because if they are not, we don't ship them." Four or five hundred guitars each year are one of a kind.

■ Like restaurants, Fender has a pricing menu for custom guitars. Custom Shop sales reps John Grunder and Mark Duncan take the base price and then add the extras. To make things easy for customers, Fender's price sheet lists the most popular options. There are at least five custom neck shapes for guitars and four for basses. But in practice, the Shop's neck duplicating machine works something like

a key maker's device and can copy any existing neck. You can order fancy bird's-eye or flame maple necks. Fretboards come in ebony, Indian rosewood, or pao ferro.

■ Customers can mix and match necks and bodies. On Stratocasters, you can interchange pickguard assemblies or drop in different pickups. Floyd Rose locking tremolo systems are available. Country rockers can get a factory original Fender with a Parsons-White B-Bender. Other choices include custom fingerboard inlays and body binding. If a customer wants an option that doesn't appear on the menu, the price is a phone call away. Any authorized Fender dealer can make an order through the Custom Shop sales department. John Page and supervisor Scott Grant make sure it can be built (they seldom have to say no). All the buyer needs is imagination and money. Not surprisingly, many of the Shop's customers, besides working musicians, are baby boomers who quit bands after high school to become well-heeled professionals in middle age.

■ Fender's Custom Shop embodies a new attitude at Fender, a company that has made a dramatic comeback by responding to its customers' needs. Several original vintage Fenders hang on the walls in Corona, including a sparkle-finish pre-CBS Telecaster Custom with black binding. To John Page, that guitar and others from its era represent a starting point. As he says, "Vintage product is something you learn from. Then you go on and design something for tomorrow." The Fender guitar was proven long ago. The Custom Shop is finding success by taking it to new heights of artistry and consistency, and by building newly designed guitars and classic jazz guitars that in the old days the company never imagined it could make. They're all Fenders. The sound and look say it all: "Yeah, this is cool. This is hip."

An Interview with Custom Shop General Manager

JOHN PAGE

by Richard R. Smith

Q: Fender guitars have become an American icon. How does the Custom Shop fit into Fender's history and legacy?

A: *I think it fits into the legacy several ways. Number one, it tries to hold up the tradition as much as possible with exact duplicates of the old guitars. Even things like the Relics are a celebration of the character of the antique collectibles. So one of the primary issues is holding on and continuing that history. At the same time, 180 degrees opposed to that, the Custom Shop can get away with taking Fender into areas where Fender as a whole cannot compete in. Whether it's in the eclectic instruments, the art instruments, the archtops, even contemporary lines of products that Fender has never been known for. The Custom Shop retains the old and helps create the new.*

Q: The original Fender factory was equipped more like a furniture shop than that of an Old World musical instrument craftsman's. Fifty years later, what's changed?

A: *We have elements of both. In some aspects, we have the crudest Old World woodworking tools available that we work with. You take somebody like a George Amicay, the wood-carver. He's just sitting there with wood chisels and an X-acto knife, carving away every day. A lot of the builders will use tools that have nothing to do with woodworking—dental tools and everything else to do inlays and things like that. But we definitely bring in more modern tools. A lot of the tools that were used originally, for instance, were the most modern woodworking tools of the day. We, the Custom Shop, probably use more of those type tools than most other guitar companies do.*

■ *We don't have a bunch of NC [numerically controlled] machines sitting around in the Custom Shop. We do utilize the NC machines that the factory has for some models. We have one small one that we do mostly tooling with…. Our whole mind-set on that—and this has been my mind-set from day one building guitars—is that*

handwork and soul and guts and everything else is so important in the guitar. But there are areas of the guitar that don't need that. You can save time, for instance, by carving out the shape of a body or the pickup chambers in the body accurately on a pin router or an NC. Then you can spend all your hand time in the way you do all the detail shaping of the body, the way you shape the neck profile, the way you dress the edges of the fretboard, the way you dress the frets, install the frets, dress the fretboard,… So, spend the most amount of time you can in the important areas by hand. And the areas that don't have to have that handwork, do it with machines.

■ *I mean, I know years ago, I was in a guitar builders' guild and going to these shows where guys would spend all year building one guitar. I'd hear, "Yeah, but I built it with one hand chisel and a beaver-tooth plane." All this kind of stuff and you're sitting here going, "Yeah, but you built one guitar. You got your family living in a Volkswagen van and wearing tapestry sandals 'cause you had to move out of your apartment to get enough money to come to this show to try to sell one guitar." I don't believe in suffering or your family suffering for your art to that level. You know what I mean? I respect them to one degree, but we can't do that.*

■ *Also, it's a modern world. You want it to be a business. If you suffer for your art and you don't make any money, then it's not business. That's not good for the customers. It's not good for the builders. It's not good for anybody. Everybody loses to me, in that instance, except maybe the artist from a spiritual point of view. He sure isn't eating, and he's living in mud somewhere. So that's always been my mentality—let the machines do what they do best, and then spend every hand detail you have to make to make it perfect.… That allows you—affords you—to do that easy.*

Q: In the nineteenth century, many guitars were considered more art objects than musical instruments. That changed when guitars became a mass-produced item, led by Fender's solidbody revolution. How do you see the paradox between what Fender used to be—the symbol of nontraditional guitar building—and what it is today—an industry leader, copied by everyone?

A: *It's not something I think about a lot. It's odd. At the same time, I think there's so many parallels in other industries, not just guitars. I'm sure Henry Ford was considered the total psycho at the time, too, being outlawed from driving the first cars around town because the horses were going wild. People probably thought he was some kind of devil worshipper or something like that because he developed this beast. Now everybody in the world makes gas-powered automobiles. The Beatles;*

they come out with a type of music, they're long-haired freaks, and next thing you know everybody in the world's trying to copy them. I think it's ironic. At the same time, I think it's normal human…humandom. That's a stupid word, but you know it's normal. It's progress. At first something's really weird, then all of a sudden somebody realizes this is really hip.

■ *You brought up earlier about Fender's founder not really being a craftsman or a guitar builder. Well, he was able to design a guitar so that he didn't have to be. If you think about it, he was the Henry Ford of the guitar. Tom Wheeler, I think, said that. It's one of the most classic quotes. Because he was able to take people who were not guitar builders, were not "luthiers," and have them build an excellent piece. So it became the perfect vehicle for people to mass-produce. I think what's interesting to me now and what I like so much about this shop now is that where Fender is a mass-produced style of instrument, we at the same time are able to take it back into the nineteenth century and do the ornate, wild, crazy stuff and kind of make full circle and get back into the art end of it as well. That's kind of neat, 'cause we always thought of Fender as the Chevy of guitars. It was always the working man's bolt-together kind of piece. And to be able to take it well beyond that has been one of our finest accomplishments.*

Q: When is a solidbody guitar an art object? Is it a 1950 Broadcaster? Is it something you make here? Or is it both?

A: *When is a Campbell's can of soup an art object? You know what I mean? Whoever thought that was art before Warhol made it? I think it's totally subjective. I think to some people, without question a 1950s Nocaster, all original, is as much a piece of art as something Michelangelo did. Other people care less about a 1950s Broadcaster and think an aluminum Harley-Davidson Strat is the most perfect piece of art there is. So a question like that can almost not be answered. It can't be argued; it's too subjective. How many times have you gone to an art museum and you stand there and you hear three other people talking about a painting and everybody thinks it's something completely different.… It's whatever you see. Art is whatever you see it to be. So I don't see any argument necessary.*

Q: Do your builders consider themselves artists, technicians, or some combination?

A: *Total combination. One nice thing about this shop is that it's not a big ego shop. You can't have artistic people and not have egos to a degree. There's no way.*

Q: It's like a band?

A: *Yeah (laughs). It's like a band. You're absolutely right. It's like a band. But if you're going to relate it like a band, it's like how do you replace Paul McCartney from the Beatles? This isn't just any band—this is Fender guitars. When you come in here, whether it's to Fender or to the Custom Shop, as the pinnacle of the Fender company, supposedly, what you're involved with is so big that it's usually pretty easy to understand in your own mind that what you are is a small part of it. Even the builders, you have your signature on the guitar. It's the most phenomenal thing that*

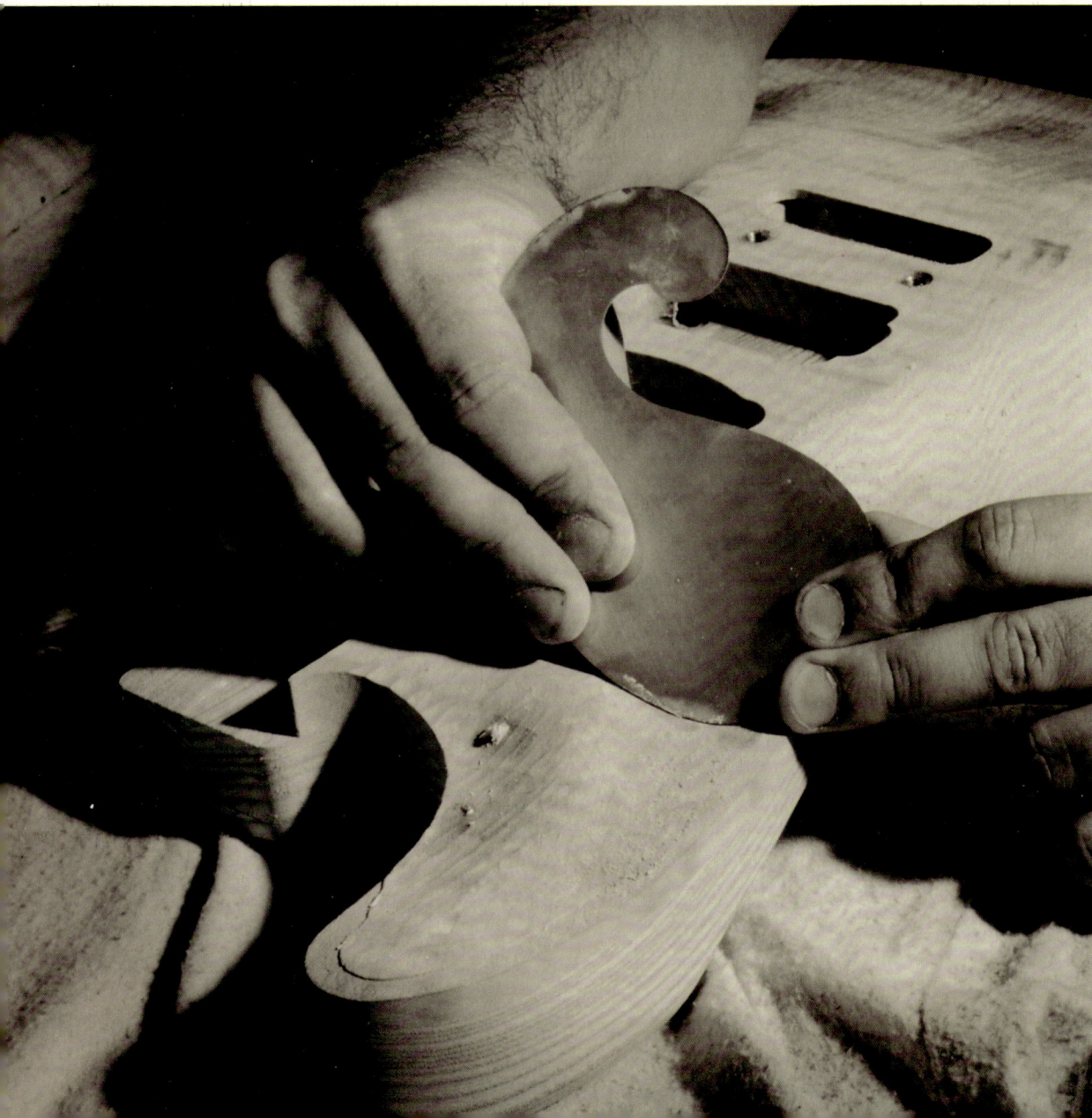

can happen to a guitar builder—have your name on that guitar. That's what it's all about. But to have Fender on the peghead, too, is like, it doesn't get any better than that to me.

■ *Most of us consider ourselves a bunch of woodworkers that happen to build guitars. Some are more artistic than others. Some guys out there—some of the best builders I've got—don't consider themselves artists one percent. J. Black is a good example. "I love building Strats, period. I don't want to design anything. I don't want to build art guitars. I love building Strats. And I love making a customer out there who orders one, thrilled to death that he gets one."*

■ *So I think it's a cross, but for the most part we're just a bunch of woodworkers that build guitars. We all hate the word "luthier," for that matter. That's too phony; no one wants to listen to that.*

Q: Is a $25,000 hand-carved Stratocaster a better musical instrument than the regular production-line model, and does that matter any more to your customers?

A: *Is a $25,000 hand-carved guitar a better guitar than another next to it? No. It's real simple: no, it's not. Is it a better guitar as a functional piece? No. But that's where art comes into play. If you're trying to cover a hole in the wall, does a 49-cent print cover the hole in the wall just as easily as the Mona Lisa? Yes. You know what I mean. If you're trying to cover a hole on the wall, then either one of those things works wonderfully. So if you're trying to play a guitar, a Custom Shop '54 Stratocaster at $2,200 retail versus a $25,000 hand-carved, inlaid-to-the-hilt kind of Stratocaster, both of them are the same when it comes to guitar function.*

Q: Are there any compromises between building a guitar that sounds great and building one that looks beautiful?

A: *There is without question a lot of factors that have to be considered when you're building a guitar. One example I always use is when a customer calls and says, "I want the fattest sounding Stratocaster, but I want it to be a solid maple body, a Floyd Rose on it, I want it to have three single-coil pickups, and I want it to have an ebony fretboard."*

■ *Okay, number one, they obviously know exactly what they want it to look like, but they also say how they want it to sound. They want it to sound fat and raunchy, and everything they just asked for will make it the thinnest guitar in the world. Usually in a situation like that you have to sit down and say, "Look, changing this material will make this sound, and changing this material will change this sound."*

■ *When we come to an art guitar, it depends on what you're trying to do. It depends on what the primary function of that piece is. If the primary function of that piece is to be a guitar that looks really bitchin', then you better damn well keep that in mind when you're designing it. That type of guitar is designed to be a playable instrument that just happens to look good.*

■ *If you're building a guitar that is without question an art object, like the Mayan guitar or something, then the art object becomes primary over playability, usually. But most of the guys out there like Fred Stuart, who has a high concentration of art guitars, and enough years under his belt to know what materials to use, can still make it sound like a really good guitar. Like the Aztec-Mayan, for instance, because* of the Corian overlays and things like that, it's a heavier guitar than I'd want to play. But I also can't believe that anyone is going to go out there and spend $75,000 for it and gig with it. Usually you go into the instrument knowing what you're looking for. If you're looking for a wall hanging—it's a piece of art—or if you're looking for a phenomenal playing guitar.

■ *The funniest thing happened to John Suhr the other day. He has a customer who has laid out exactly how he wanted his guitar: hand-wind the pickups, do all these kind of things. Make this killer guitar. He was talking with the customer before he shipped it, because the customer was thinking about changing his mind on the pickups—which pickups he had just had hand-wound. And at the end of the entire conversation, the guy says, "You know what, it probably doesn't matter, because I'm probably just going to hang it on my wall anyway." And John says that it's going to be a great guitar. It's going to play wonderfully, it's going to sound wonderfully. If you want to hang it on the wall, fine, but trust me—it's a player. It's weird, because usually you know what the customer is going to do with the instrument.*

Q: Do people custom-order a sound over a look?

A: Yeah. In fact that's what we do on every order. The builder talks to every customer. The most important part of that conversation is, "What kind of sound are you looking for? What kind of playing style do you have? What are your influences?" So the builder knows as much as possible what that customer is looking for, because the most important thing to the builder is obviously the sound. The art is fine. The art is icing—big-time icing on this cake that we're in the middle of. But the cake, the meat and potatoes, whatever you want to say, the crutch of the whole thing is what the guitar sounds like. And yeah, going back to that example I used before, where the guy says I want this, this, and this, and I want it to be fat, but I want all these bright-sounding objects. We'll usually sit down with a customer like that and say, "Okay now, this is great. It's a beautiful guitar, but it's not going to sound fat. What's important to you? If that tone is really important to you, we can get close to the aesthetics by doing this. We can give you a nice maple top but maybe on a medium ash body or an alder body. And maybe instead

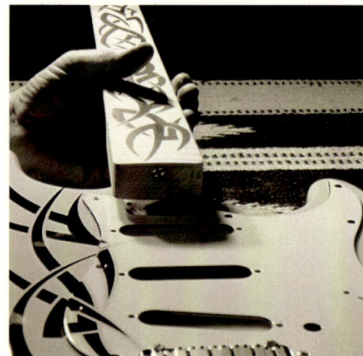

of a Floyd, we go to the Floyd-Blanda, a locking system but not as massive, and maybe an LSR [ball bearing] nut or a roller nut or some type of locking gears or Teflon nut." We'll always steer it back to that tone if the guy is asking for the aesthetics. If the guy's asking for tone, we usually know exactly what to do. I'd say 70 percent of our players are more tone oriented than aesthetics oriented.

Q: Fred Stuart told me that many customers want what they see in pictures—that they trust the craftsman's and artist's judgment when they order a guitar. How often do customers come to you with well-thought-out designs? Do they know exactly what they want, or do they want you guys to be the facilitators?

A: *Well, it depends on how you define "design." We have very few people who come to us with a design like an Aztec-Mayan or a White Buffalo or a Western Boot Set. We don't have people come to us with ideas like that. We do have people all the time come with specifics of how they want their Strat or how they want their Tele to be done—what kind of pickups, what kind of wood, how they want the contour on the body, how they want the profile on the neck, how they want the back of the peghead shaped. We get that quite often. I'd say probably nine times out of ten those are the vintage-type collectors. Those are the guys who have actually had that guitar, or remember that guitar because they used to have it, and they're going from memory. And they get very, very specific.*

basis of the shop. Where we'll be in five years is where the music leaders will be in five years. Where the musicians are in five years, that's where we'll be. If the musicians change where they're at tomorrow from where they are today, we're going to be there the day after tomorrow. In five years...we want to be right on where this industry is then. I see the Custom Shop continuing to do everything possible to nail the past, to do even better to nail the past—the great of the past; let the chaff fall away. And I also see us continuing to push the future along. So I see us being what we are today, but just more of it. I don't see us being bigger. I do see us being better.

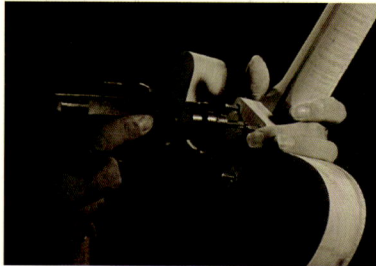

THE MASTER BUILDERS

FRED STUART

"Twang!" That says it all for me! My earliest recollections of music are some of the old hillbilly artists from the mid fifties. When I found out that the best sounds were being made on Telecasters, I was irrevocably converted.

■ Being a part of the process of carrying on the tradition is no less than an honor and a privilege.

J.W. BLACK

After nearly two decades of guitar building, I find that every day a new idea or challenge comes along and engages me into the art, mystery, skill, and passion that I enjoy for my livelihood.

■ The ultimate experience is having 50 years of Fender history peering over your shoulder as you string up a new instrument for the first time—meeting the challenge of the Fender legacy.

■ Day in, day out, there could not be a better job.·

JOHN ENGLISH

I was born in California in the 1950s, and I was introduced to music at a young age. I started playing drums in 1962 and played in bands until 1965, when my family moved to Europe.

■ While in Europe I missed my music, so I bought a guitar; this started it all. I started working on guitars in the sixties, and it has been my life ever since.

■ After returning from Europe I worked with a few bands until 1972, when I went to work for Fender.

■ My favorite guitars have always been Fenders, including the Telecaster and Stratocaster. I have also been interested in archtop guitars, especially those from the twenties and thirties.

■ I feel quite honored to work at the finest shop in the industry.

ALAN HAMEL

For the past 20 years I've made a living with a guitar in my hands, either playing, repairing, or making them. I've seen trends and fads come and go about how this or that gadget will make you faster, louder, play in tune better, or give you more sustain, highs, or lows.

■ I'm proud to be a part of the process that builds the guitars that have withstood the hype and continue to be the instruments all others are judged by.

STEPHEN
STERN

I grew up in the sixties and
seventies, when the music
scene was very exciting.
I knew I wanted to be
involved in the music business. I have always had a
love for guitars and also for
woodworking. Therefore,
becoming a guitar builder
seemed like a natural career
choice for me.

■ Working for Fender
Custom Shop affords me
the opportunity to do
something I love and have
the freedom to be creative.

JOHN SUHR

During my senior year of high school in New Jersey, I built my first guitar, with some major assistance from Bob Benedetto. Bob moved to Florida. I needed some inlay work and a fret job done on the blank ebony fretboard. I decided to take my favorite and only guitar to 48th Street in New York City to have this work done. Four months of phone calls later I finally got my guitar back, basically destroyed, irreparable—chipped fingerboard, terrible fret job—totally butchered! That was the day 21 years ago that I decided that I could and would take on any guitar repairs and building myself.

■ Working at Fender, for the first time in my life I feel that I am in control of the guitars I build. I am given the freedom to build custom instruments using methods I am comfortable with. I no longer need to rely on outside sources for parts or paint. I'm happy to be a part of Fender history.

MARK KENDRICK

I consider myself very fortunate and blessed at the same time. Being born in the late fifties into a musical family, I began playing guitar at age five. My father and uncle, who were both working musicians at the time, played with Bob Wills, Red Foley, Marty Robbins, and countless others. This afforded me tremendous influences when I was young.

■ When not on the road, my uncle (Buddy Kendrick) worked with Fender and CLF. Consequently, I always had Fender guitars around. When I was old enough to handle a screwdriver I began to tear them apart and reassemble them. If I ran into a problem, my uncle or my father would take them back to Freddie Tavares or Gene Fields and have them put back together. So I learned guitar building literally hands on, and indirectly from "The" masters.

■ I feel very honored and proud to carry on a family legacy and to be part of such a wonderful organization. I can honestly say it's a pleasure to get up and come to work in the morning.

GENE BAKER

It always seemed like I could never afford that guitar in the window, so I began making bodies in seventh-grade woodshop class and fitting them with after-market parts and necks that I found at local shops. This spurred on an overwhelming indulgence for knowledge of guitars, woods, electronics, design concepts, etc., in the quest for the ultimate guitar. As I grew older, playing and enjoying different music styles, I realized that there is no one perfect guitar and began to enjoy how different guitars are suited for different sounds and styles. The Strat always seemed to be the most versatile, due to the fact that it's so easy to modify, whether it's necks, bodies, electronics, and yet it's so comfortable to play.

■ Being a master builder helps bring all my talents into play, since our one-off orders range from the simplest reproductions to the radically bizarre, leaving it up to the imagination of the customer and the skill and knowledge of the builder to turn these ideas into a beautiful, musical, and forever enjoyable instrument.

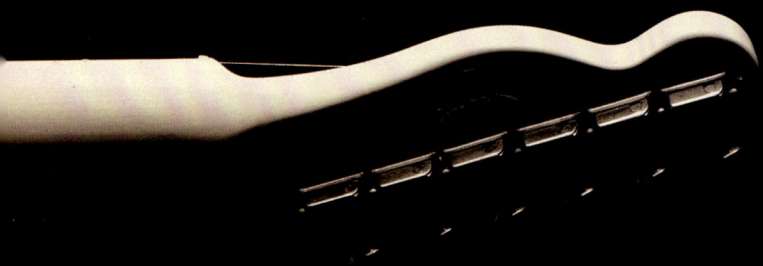

"FIRST BREATH" STRATOCASTER

Designed By:
Wyland and George Amicay

Built By:
Custom Shop Staff

Relief carving and
inlay — George Amicay

Painting — Wyland

An original hand painting by
world-renowned artist Wyland
adorns this alder relief-carved
body. The highly figured
bird's-eye blue stained maple
neck with ebony fingerboard
is accented with sterling silver
Wyland jewelry. The guitar is
accessorized with genuine
abalone and chrome.

Courtesy of Stephen Monaco and
St. Charles Guitar Exchange,
St. Charles, MO

Alan Hamel

Carving — George Amicay

Silver work — Alan Hamel

Engraving — Miles Haworth

Highly flamed maple tops with western silhouettes relief-carved on solid alder bodies. Hand-twisted sterling silver barbed wire inlay. Hair-on calf-skin pickguards, hand-engraved hardware. Bird's-eye maple necks with pau ferro fretboards and hand-twisted sterling silver inlay.

Courtesy of Corner Music, Nashville, TN

Designed By:
Fred Stuart and George Amicay

Built By:
Fred Stuart

Carving — George Amicay

Made with DuPont Corian*
on ash and maple. Carved
and inlaid with Egyptian motif.

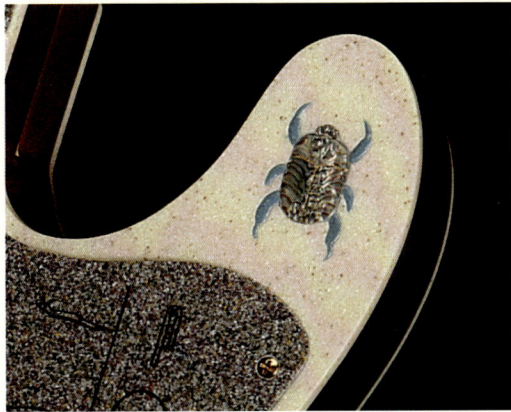

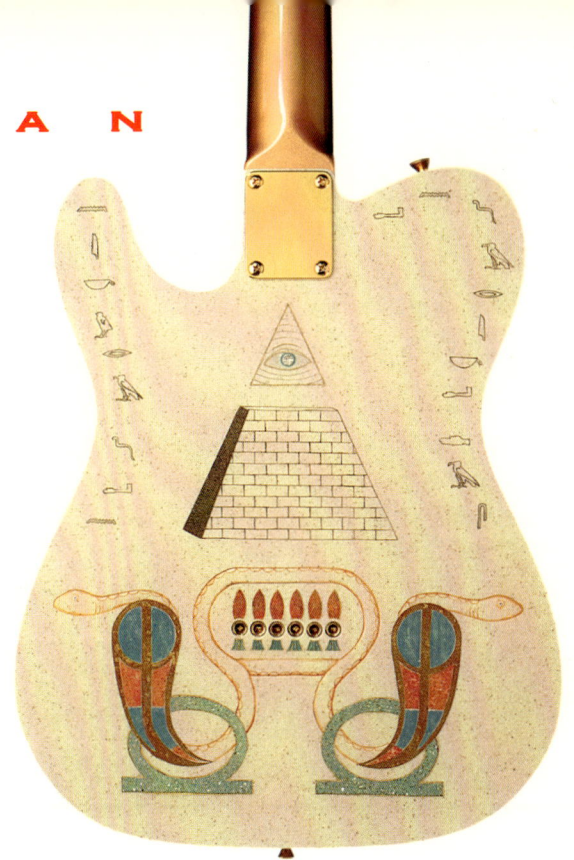

* Corian is a trademark of DuPont

Courtesy of Kirk Sand,
Guitar Shoppe, Laguna Beach, CA

Designed By:

Kurt Cobain and Larry Brooks

Built By:

Larry Brooks

A combination of Jaguar and Mustang guitars.

Courtesy of Fender Museum Collection

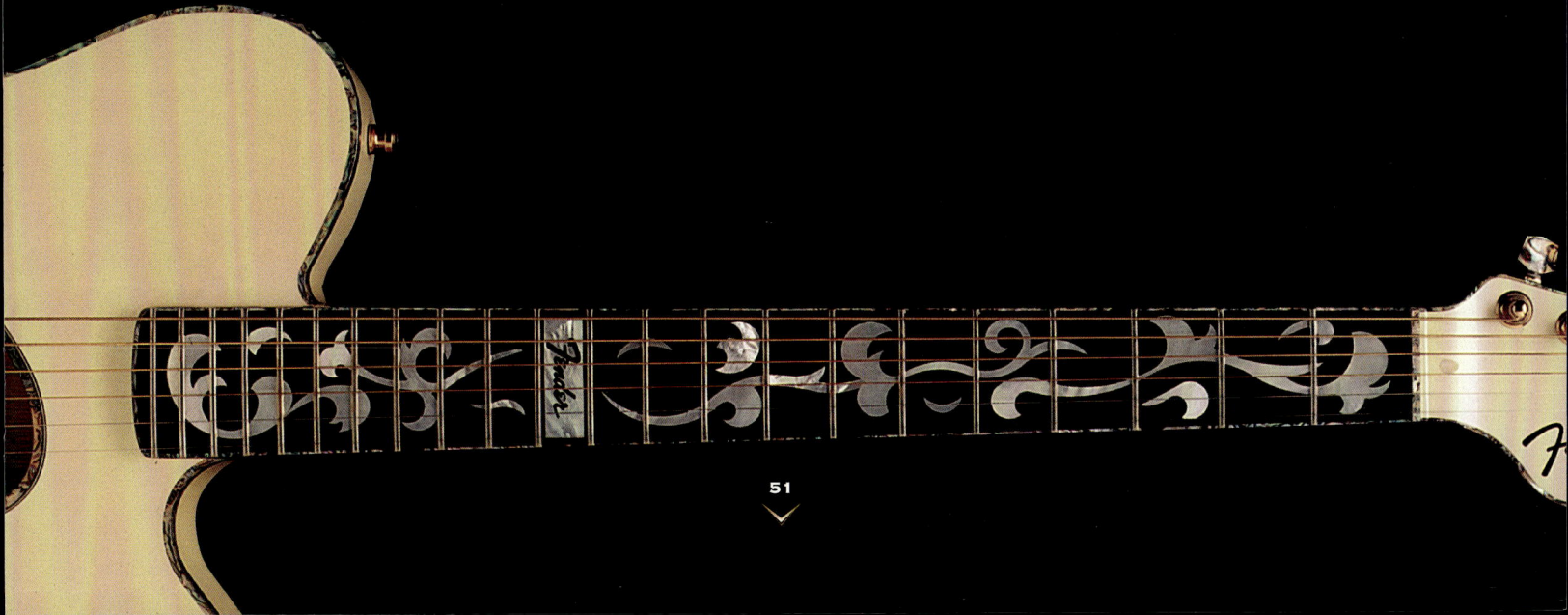

A L O H A

Designed By:
John English

Built By:
John English

Engraving — Ron Chacey

Color anodizing — Peter Kellett

Hand-engraved aluminum body with selective color anodizing. Flame maple neck. Custom aluminum headstock overlay, engraved and colorized.

Courtesy of Fender Germany

WAYLON JENNINGS TRIBUTE

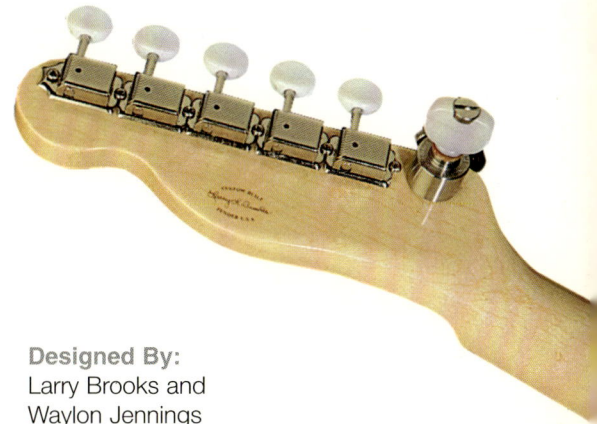

Designed By:
Larry Brooks and
Waylon Jennings

Built By:
Custom Shop Staff

Leather inlay —
Dru WhiteFeather

Neck inlay — George Amicay

Black double-bound Telecaster
with leather inlay. "Flying W" logo
on maple neck.

Courtesy of Waylon Jennings

Designed By:
John English

Built By:
John English

Oversized figured maple Telecaster body and neck. Ebony fretboard with white and black mother-of-pearl twelfth-fret marker. Top is spruce with multi-binding, and the neck is set to the body.

Courtesy of Dan Smith

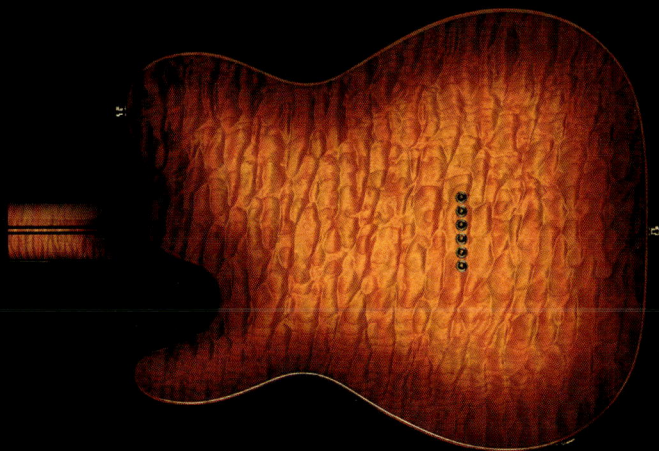

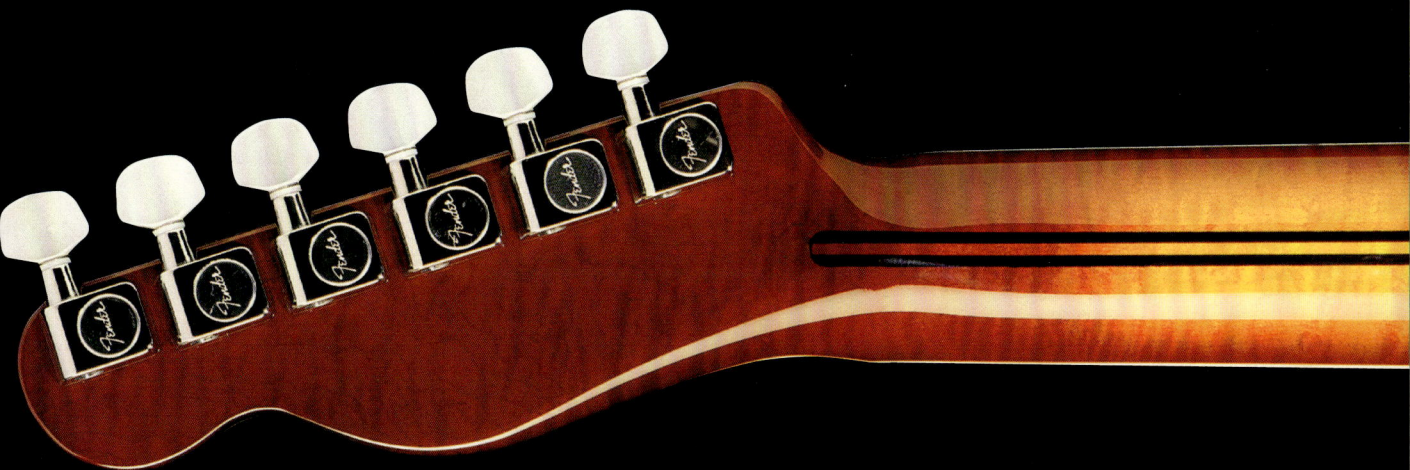

DWEEZIL ZAPPA
SPARKLE F-HOLE STRAT

Designed By:
Dweezil Zappa and J.W. Black

Built By:
J.W. Black

Thinline Strat in alder, with a maple neck. The entire instrument is finished in silver metal-flake.

Courtesy of Dweezil Zappa

BLACK LIMBA
TRIPLE SET

Gene Baker

Three-piece matching set built of black limba necks and bodies, with rosewood fretboards.

Courtesy of Fender Museum Collection

WESTERN BOOT SET

Designed By:
Alan Hamel and
Nicholas Gutierrez

Built By:
Alan Hamel

Leather work — Alan Hamel,
Nicholas Gutierrez/Renicks Boots

Engraving — Miles Haworth

Silver work — Alan Hamel

Calfskin-laced, four-color kidskin
leather-covered solid alder body with
western boots, belt, and strap to match.
Hand-engraved hardware, custom
pickups. The bird's-eye maple neck
has a pau ferro fretboard featuring
hand-twisted sterling silver and jeweler's
bronze wire inlay and sterling silver
headstock overlay.

Courtesy of Robert Galassi,
Ossining Music, Ossining, NY

DECO SPARKLE STRAT

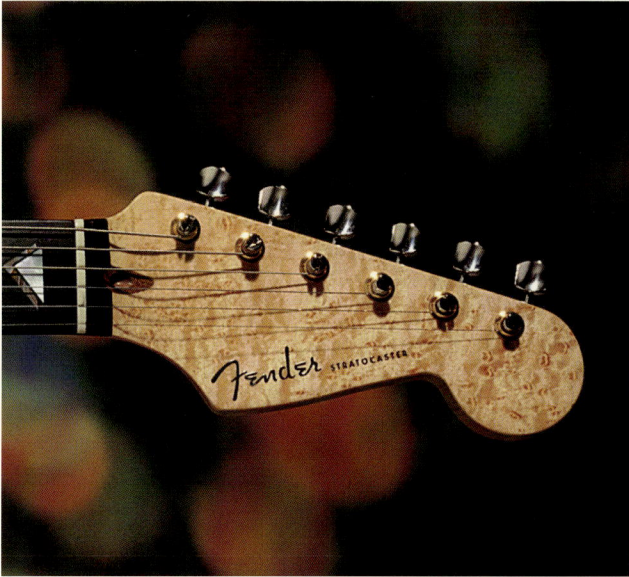

Designed By:
J.W. Black

Built By:
J.W. Black

Inlay — Tom Ellis

Silver and gold holo-flake mix with ebony fretboard. Gold and nickel parts with Texas Special pickups and metal covers.

Courtesy of Scott Leibow

Designed By:

Danny Gatton, Fred Stuart, and
Alan Hamel

Built By:

Alan Hamel and Fred Stuart

Ash body with maple necks. One guitar
neck and one six-string bass. A right-
and left-handed tremolo and gold
anodized pickguard.

Courtesy of the Gatton family

WHITE BUFFALO
"MIRACLE"

Designed By:
Dru WhiteFeather

Built By:
Neck and inlay —
George Amicay

Silver, leather, and hand bead
work — Dru WhiteFeather

Assembly — Jason Davis

Hand-painted Hopi kachina —
Sheree Henry

An ash body covered in
deerskin. An elkskin gig bag
with a Pendleton blanket lining.
Glass seed beads. Sterling
silver hardware with traditional
silver stamping. Turquoise and
mother-of-pearl inlay.

Courtesy of Alan Levin,
Washington Music, Wheaton, MD

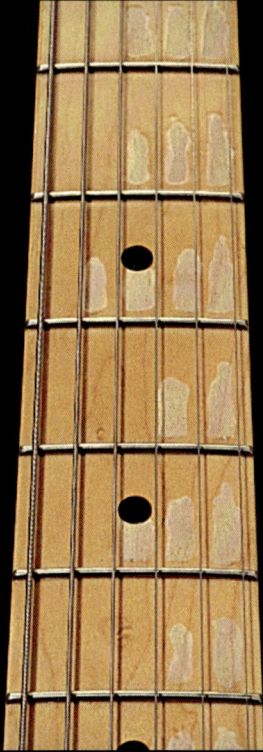

J.W. Black, Vince Cunetto, and Custom Shop Staff

Re-creation of Fender fifties classic with a "played in" appearance.

Courtesy of Fender Museum Collection

RELIC: '56
MARY KAYE STRAT

Built By:

J.W. Black, Vince Cunetto, and Custom Shop Staff

Re-creation of Fender fifties classic with a "played in" appearance.

Courtesy of Fender Museum Collection

Fred Stuart and Larry Robinson

Fred Stuart

Inlay — Larry Robinson

Made with DuPont Corian*, featuring a substrate of ash for the body and maple for the neck. Inlaid with an Aztec/Mayan motif in pearl, abalone, plastic, and various metals.

* Corian is a trademark of DuPont

Courtesy of Fender Museum Collection

Designed By:
James L. D'Aquisto

Built By:
Stephen Stern

Hand-carved spruce top and flame maple back. Figured maple neck with ebony fretboard and pearl fret markers. Vintage fifties Alnico V pickup, gold-plated and ebony hardware, with an aged blonded finish.

Courtesy of Guitar Center,
Arlington Heights, IL

HARLEY-DAVIDSON 90TH ANNIVERSARY COMMEMORATIVE STRATOCASTER

John Page, J.W. Black, and Pamelina H.

Scott Buehl and Jason Davis

Inlay — PEARLWORKS

Engraving — Louis Alegre

Hand-engraved Harley-Davidson celebratory art on a custom-made aluminum body and pickguard. Selectively plated in chrome and gold. Highly figured maple neck with an ebony fretboard and stainless steel fret markers.

Courtesy of Fender Museum Collection

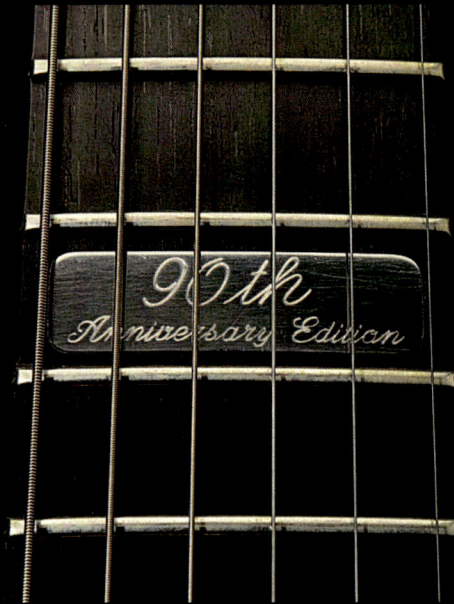

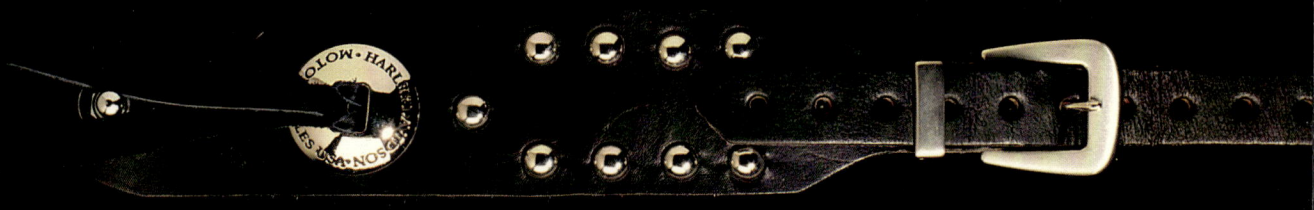

CARVED FLORAL STRATOCASTER

Designed By:
George Amicay

Built By:
Custom Shop Staff

Relief carving — George Amicay

A contrasting flame maple top, relief-carved with a traditional western floral design, adorns this mahogany body and neck. It is accented with gold appointments, pau ferro fingerboard, and abalone fret markers.

Courtesy of Fender Museum Collection

J.W. Black

Custom Shop Staff

Inlay — Bill Swank and Larry Sifel

One-piece figured maple body.
Highly figured neck with pau ferro
fingerboard featuring an inlaid
tree of life. Custom twenty-nine-
piece run.

Courtesy of Bill Schultz

PINK FLAMINGO

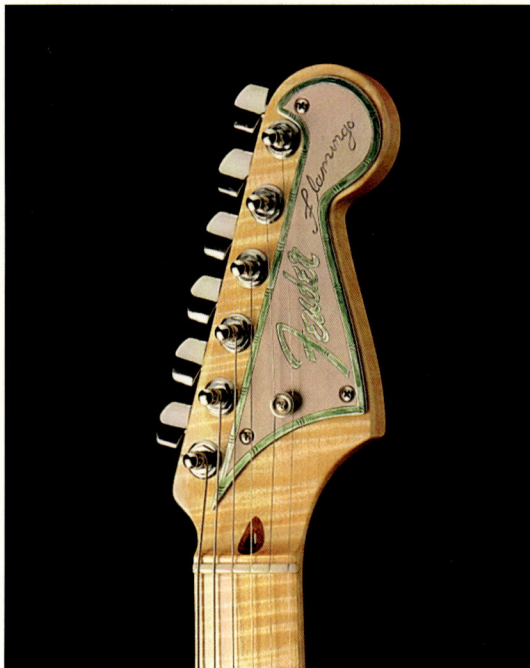

Designed By:
John English

Built By:
John English

Engraving — Ron Chacey

Color anodizing — Peter Kellett

An aluminum body, engraved and color anodized. Highly figured flame maple neck with headstock overlay. Pink moto position markers and custom-made aluminum knobs, switch tip, and pickup covers.

Courtesy of Fender Museum Collection

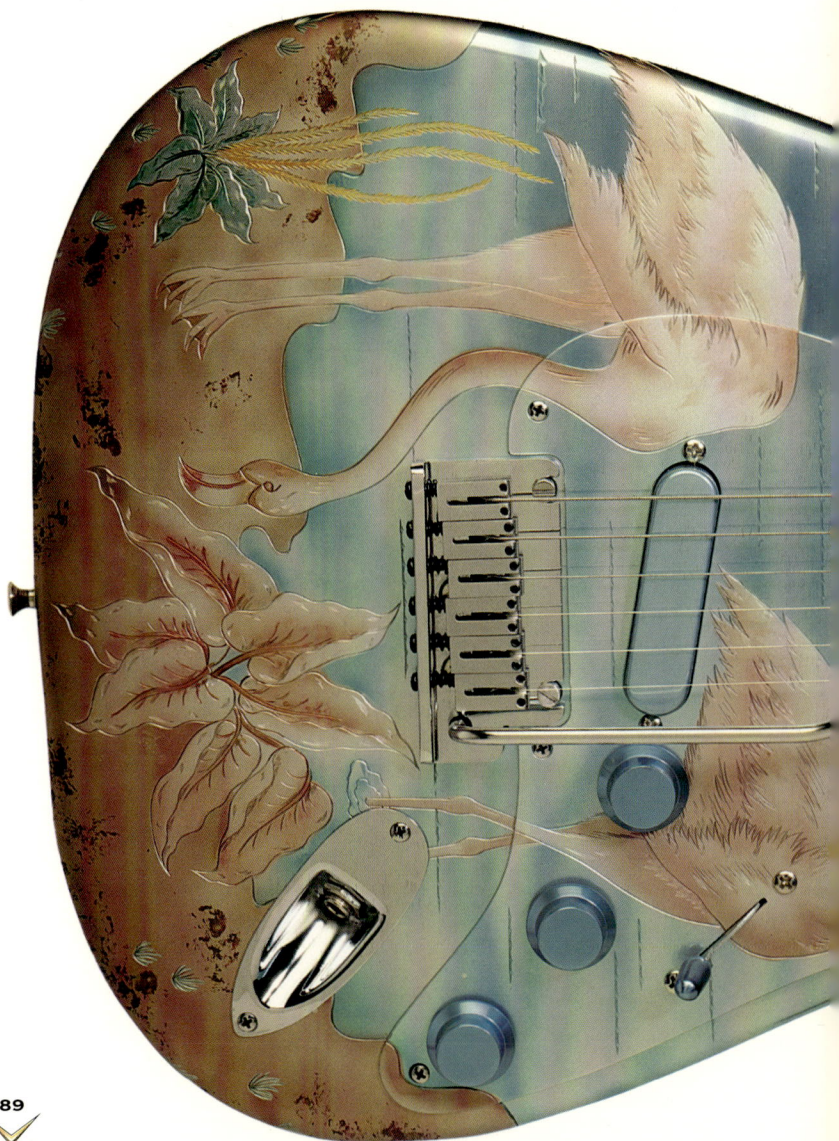

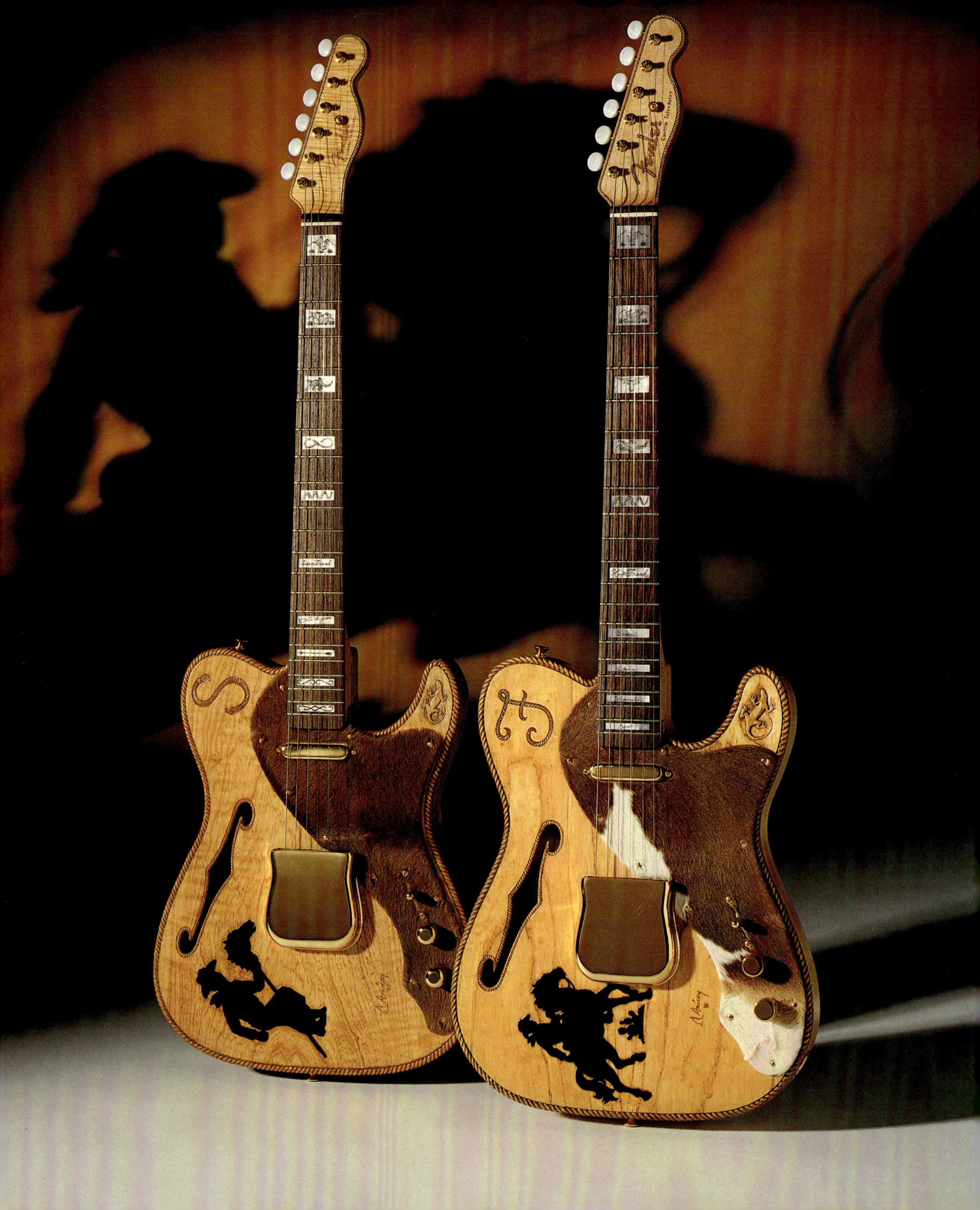

FATHER AND SON
COWBOY TELE SET

George Amicay, Kip Frank, and J.W. Black

J.W. Black and John English

Carving and inlay —
George Amicay

Adult and child Thinline Telecasters with custom inlay and carving in a cowboy motif.

Courtesy of Kip and Sean Frank

Designed By:
George F. Blanda Jr.

Built By:
George F. Blanda Jr.

Paint — Alfredo Esquival

Body style reminiscent of American cars from the mid fifties. Features hand-formed chrome trim, modified '58 Oldsmobile knobs, and a modified Jazzmaster tremolo.

Courtesy of Private Collector

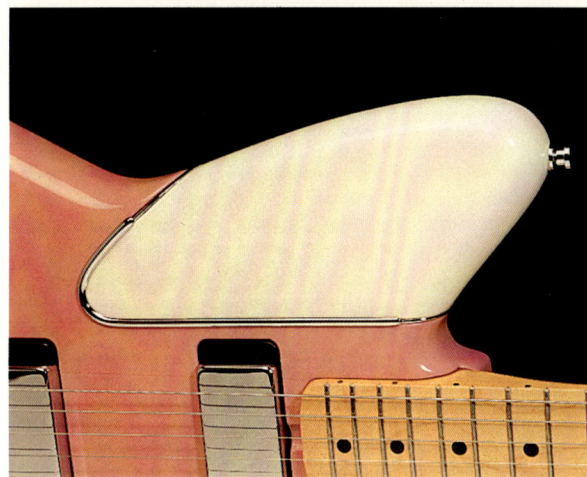

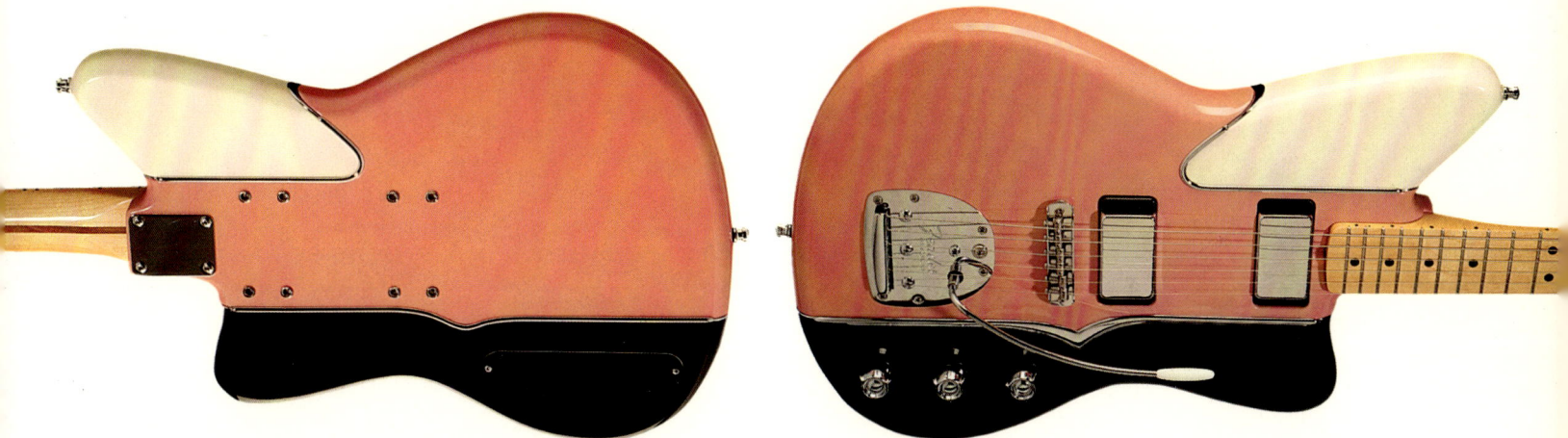

Built by
Fred Stuart

Replica of a guitar built as one of a matching set for Buck Owens and Don Rich in 1963. This guitar features a gold metal-flake finish with checkerboard binding and a maple-on-maple neck with matching peghead.

Courtesy of Matt Umanov, Umanov Guitars, New York, NY

Built By:

J.W. Black

Inlay — Tom Ellis

Bodies are quilted maple on ash. Bound necks with abalone blocks. EMG pickups with a preamp by John Suhr.

Courtesy of Fender Museum Collection

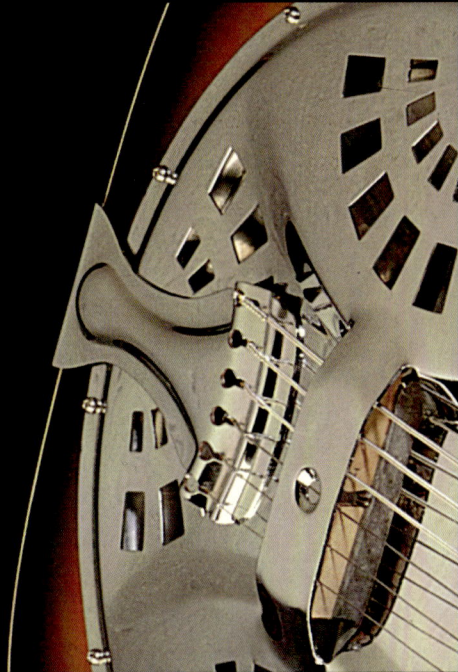

Fred Stuart

Fred Stuart

This guitar is carved from two solid pieces of ash — a top and a back — glued together, with a one-piece neck set up for playing slide.

Courtesy of Private Collector

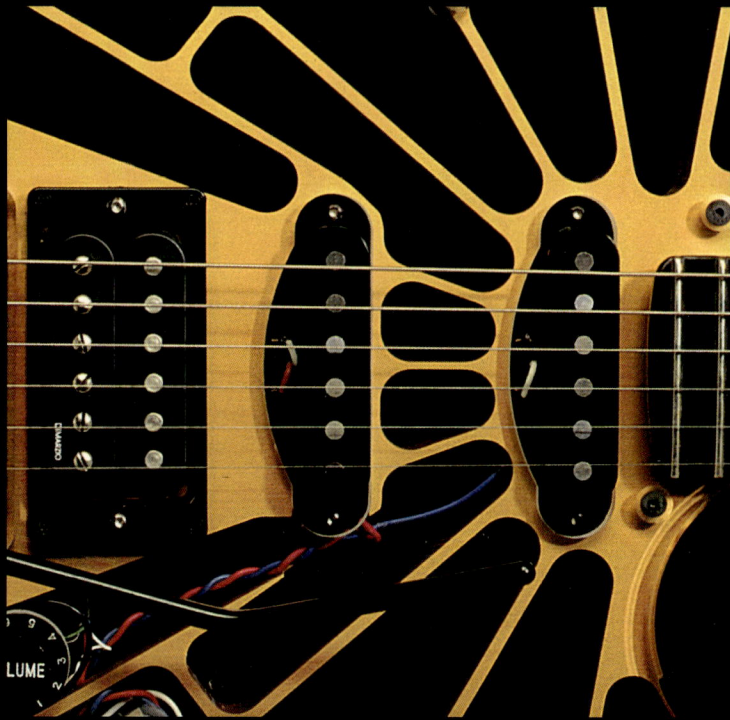

Designed By:
S.J. Boulanger

Built By:
Steve Boulanger and John English

Three-piece body: front and back of shaped and polished clear acrylic, middle milled out of aircraft aluminum and gold anodized. The neck is figured maple with ebony fingerboard.

Courtesy of Private Collector

Designed By:
John Page, Pamelina H., Gene Baker, and Larry Robinson

Built By:
Gene Baker

Inlay — Larry Robinson

Painting — Pamelina H.

Picture frame — John Page

Inlaid bird of fire on a semi-hollow quilted mahogany carved-top Strat. Quilted mahogany set neck with pau ferro fretboard.

Courtesy of Fender Museum Collection

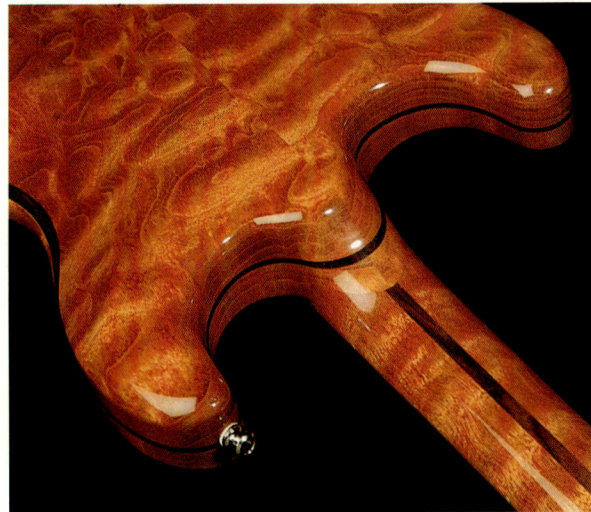

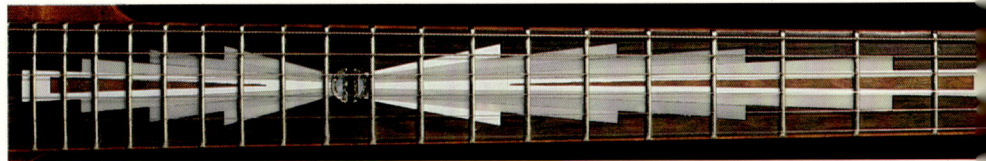

Fred Stuart and Bill Rich

Fred Stuart

Left-handed body and neck
built to be played right-handed.

Courtesy of Bill Rich, Tulsa, OK

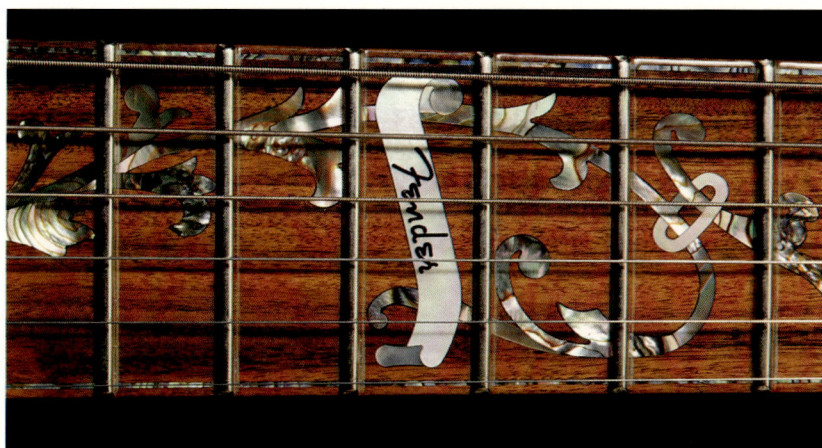

Designed By:
J.W. Black and Larry Sifel

Built By:
J.W. Black

Inlay — Larry Sifel

Pau ferro neck with abalone "tree of life" inlay and border. Flame koa on bird's-eye alder body with abalone vine throughout.

Courtesy of Larry Sifel and Fender Museum Collection

Designed By:
John English, George Amicay, and John Page

Built By:
Custom Shop Staff

Inlay — Larry Sifel, PEARLWORKS

Engraving — Ron Chacey

Hand-engraved Hawaiian art on a custom-made aluminum body. The neck is made of highly figured wood with custom inlay on both fingerboard and headstock.

Courtesy of Fender Museum Collection

DRAGON WITH MERMAID

Designed By:
George Amicay

Built By:
John English

Painting — Pamelina H.

Relief carving — George Amicay

A bas-relief-carved dragon and mermaid adorn this hand-painted solid alder body, accented by genuine mother-of-pearl teeth and an abalone eye. The neck is bird's-eye maple with a hand-painted, relief-carved woman's profile at the headstock.

Courtesy of Fender Museum Collection

Fred Stuart and George Amicay

Fred Stuart

Leather work —
Dru WhiteFeather

Carving — George Amicay

Ash Thinline body carved and
inlaid with rhinestones. Maple-
on-maple neck carved and
filled with acrylic.

Courtesy of Yamano Music, Japan

Designed By:
Larry Robinson and Fred Stuart

Built By:
Fred Stuart

Inlay — Larry Robinson

Decorative gilding — Lil Louie

Made with DuPont Corian*
on ash and maple. Inlaid
with pearl, abalone, and
various metals.

* Corian is a trademark of DuPont

Courtesy of Fender Museum Collection

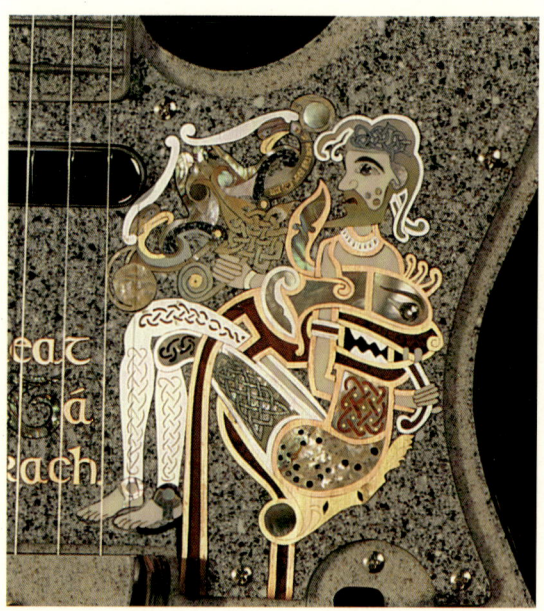

Designed By:

Fred Stuart and George Amicay

Built By:

Fred Stuart

Carving — George Amicay

Made with DuPont Corian* on ash and maple. The vines were hand-carved and gilded with 24-karat gold. The leaves and grapes are inlaid rhinestones.

* Corian is a trademark of DuPont

Courtesy of Fender Museum Collection

Designed By:
Fred Stuart and George Amicay

Built By:
Fred Stuart

Carving — George Amicay

Ash Thinline body featuring a rope carved around the upper half. Rosewood-on-maple neck with block inlay. Tooled leather pickguard.

Courtesy of Guitar Center, Hollywood, CA

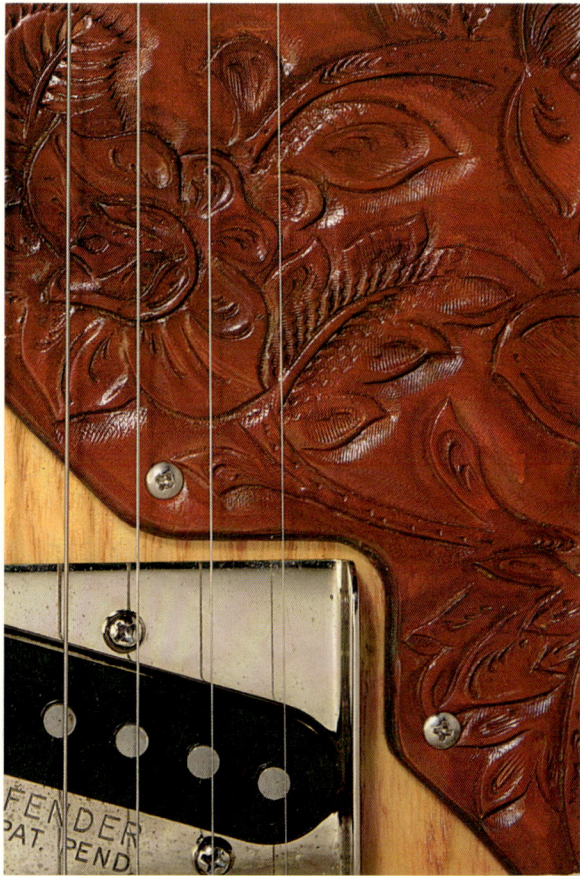

Designed By:

John Page,
Pamelina H., and
Jim Petersen from
PLAYBOY

Built By:

Custom Shop Staff

Painting —
Pamelina H.

Inlay — Larry Sifel,
PEARLWORKS

Hand-painted Marilyn
Monroe centerfold on
a solid alder body.
Highly figured maple
neck with Playboy
"bunny head" fret
markers in black pearl.

Courtesy of
Fender Museum Collection

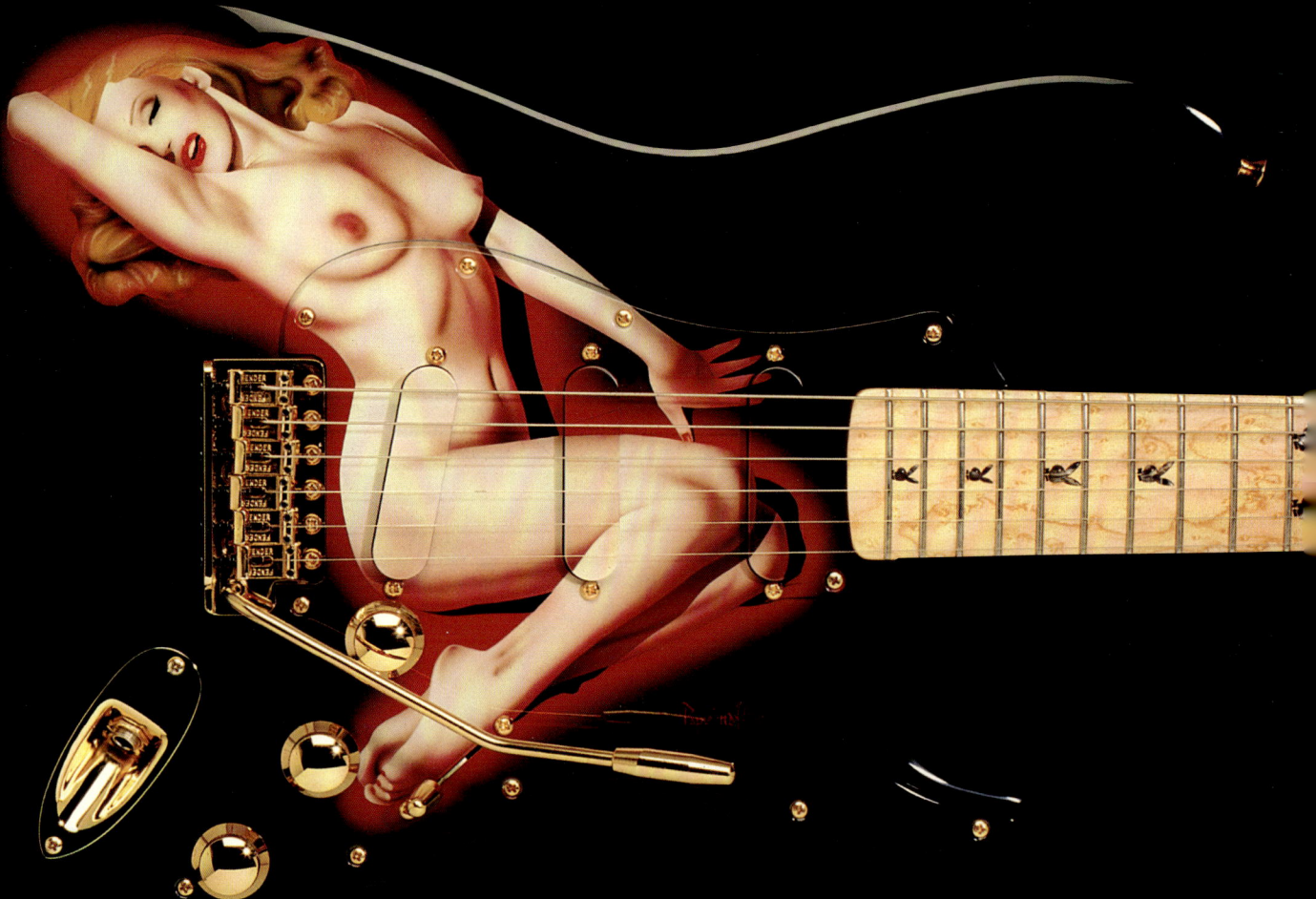

Designed by:
Gene Baker, John Suhr, and
John Page

Built By:
Gene Baker

Ash body, highly figured maple
carved top. Highly figured maple neck
with abalone position markers.

Courtesy of Dan Martin,
St. Charles Guitar Exchange, St. Charles, MO

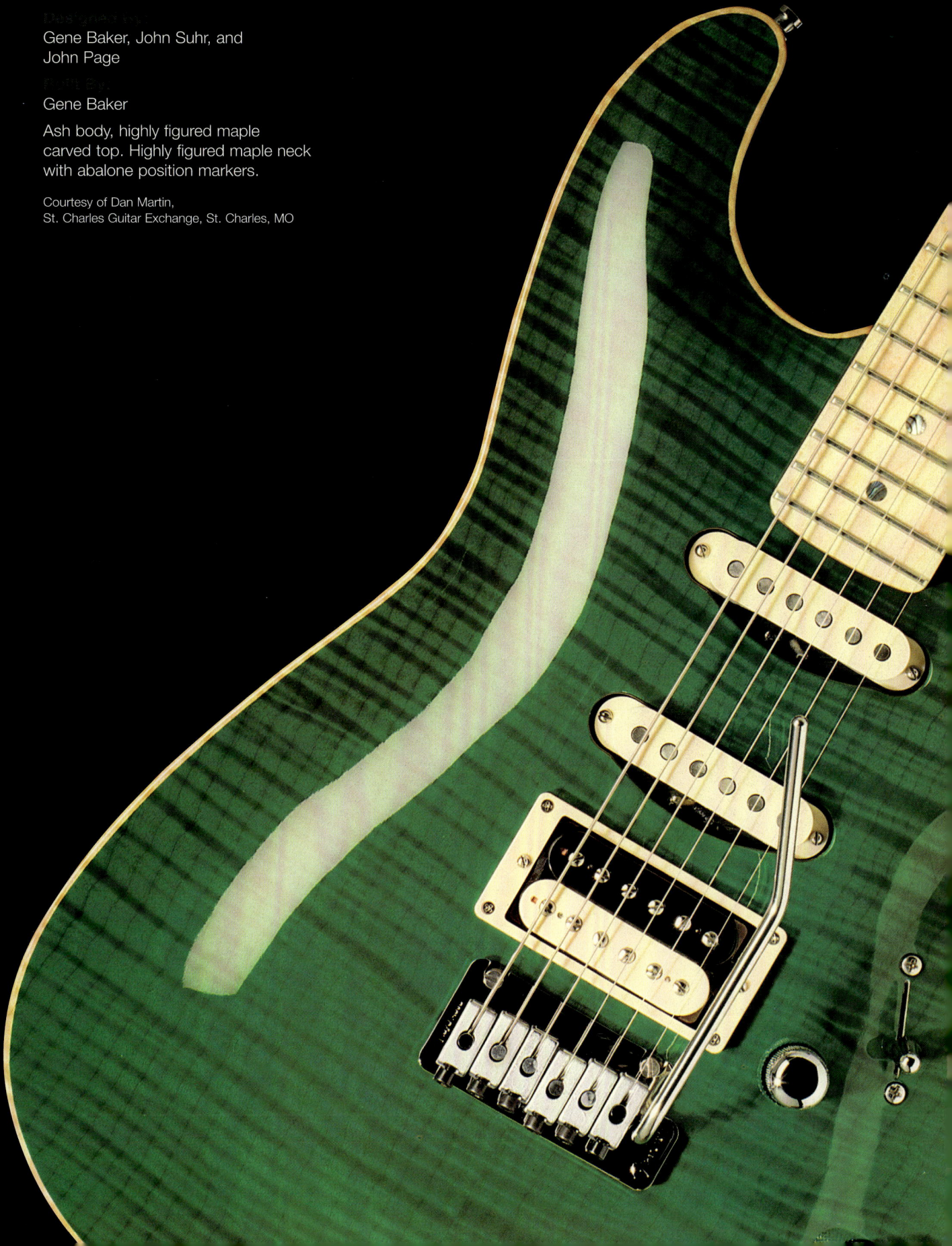

1993 NAMM METAL
ENGRAVED STRATOCASTER

Designed By:
J.W. Black and Ron Chacey

Built By:
J.W. Black

Body engraving and fingerboard
inlay — Ron Chacey

Metal body with Art Nouveau
engraving. Custom neck inlay. First
metal engraved guitar shown at
NAMM and produced by the
Custom Shop.

Courtesy of Gary Moline,
Guitar Center, Hollywood, CA

Designed By:

J.W. Black, John Page, and Pamelina H.

Built By:

Custom Shop Staff

Engraved pickguard — Ron Chacey

Twelfth fret inlay — Larry Sifel

Two-tone sunburst flame maple top on ash body. Hand-engraved gold-plated pickguard. Highly figured maple neck with inlaid block and "1954–1994" banner at the twelfth fret. Gold leaf "Fender" and "40th" logos.

Ring included with guitar.

Courtesy of Fender Museum Collection

Designed By:
Courtney Love and Larry Brooks

Built By:
Larry Brooks and Mark Kendrick

Custom body shape with bound rosewood neck.

Courtesy of Fender Museum Collection

CHECKERBOARD
BAJO SEXTO TELECASTER

Designed By:
Fred Stuart

Built By:
Fred Stuart

Red sparkle Telecaster with a
checkerboard design.

Courtesy of Rick Nielsen

Fred Stuart and John Page

Fred Stuart

Painting — Pamelina H.

Ash vintage-style Telecaster covered with black velvet and featuring a black-and-gold rope inlay.

Courtesy of Fender Museum Collection

THE KING LIVES!

**Fender Electric Spanish
Guitar — Prototype (1949)
"Professional" Amp (1946)**

Built By:

Guitar — Fred Stuart
and John Page

Amp — Bruce Zinky, Bill Giles,
John Page, and Steve Murillo

Flight cases — Bob Morris,
Holmberg Cases

Form-fit case — Jerry Germain,
G&G Quality Case

Guitar: Pine body with maple
neck. No truss rod.

Amp: Figured maple cabinet.

Both the guitar and the amp
replicate the originals as closely
as possible.

Courtesy of Fender Museum Collection

Tony Franklin
The Firm, Blue Murder, Paul Rodgers

Audley Freed*
Cry of Love

Eric Gales*

James Garver*
Garth Brooks

Danny Gatton*

Janick Gers*
Iron Maiden

Billy Gibbons
ZZ Top

Tony Gilkyson
X

Vince Gill

David Gilmour*
Pink Floyd

Glenn Gordon
Mark Chesnutt

Green Day*

Buddy Guy*

Tom Hamilton
Aerosmith

Stu Hamm*
Joe Satriani, Steve Vai

Kirk Hammett
Metallica

David Harris*
Dionne Farris

Steve Harris*
Iron Maiden

Jeff Healey*

Dusty Hill
ZZ Top

Corky Holbrook
Billy Ray Cyrus

Joe Holmes*
Ozzy Osbourne

Michael Houser*
Widespread Panic

Greg Howe*

Porter Howell
Little Texas

Jan Ianemkov
Gorky Park

Billy Idol

Colin James*

Waylon Jennings*

Eric Johnson

Jimmy Johnson
Vince Gill

John Jorgenson
Desert Rose Band

Ivan Julian*
Matthew Sweet

Henry Kaiser
French-Frith-Kaiser-Frisell

Pat Kelly
George Benson, Tom Scott

Mike Keneally*
Frank Zappa

Kentucky Headhunters*

Tony King*
Brooks & Dunn

Danny Kortchmar

Richie Kotzen*
Poison

Lenny Kravitz

Sonny Landreth

Little Feat*

Live

Lisa Loeb Band*

Los Lobos*

Courtney Love & Hole

Andy Low
Eric Clapton

Yngwie Malmsteen*

Mick Mars
Mötley Crüe

Wolf Marshall*

Eddie Martinez

Hank Marvin
The Shadows

Terry McBride
McBride & the Ride

Steve McClure*
Garth Brooks

Rick McCrae
George Strait

Mike McCready
Pearl Jam

Duff McKagan
Guns N' Roses

John McVie*
Fleetwood Mac

Michelle Meldrum*
Phantom Blue

*Denotes Fender Endorsee

Sean Michael*
Dionne Farris

The Mighty Mighty Bosstones*

Blue Miller
Gibson-Miller Band

Don Mock
Instructor—GIT

Ian Moore*

Vinnie Moore*

Alanis Morissette Band*

James Murphy*
Testament

Dave Murray
Iron Maiden

Dave Navarro*
Red Hot Chili Peppers

No Use for a Name*

Aldo Nova

Barry Oakley Jr.
Bloodline

Ben Orr
The Cars

The Outlaws*

Buck Owens

Jimmy Page
Led Zeppelin

Phil Palmer
Eric Clapton

Lee Roy Parnell*

Dolly Parton

Joe Perry
Aerosmith

Ricky Phillips*
Bad English

Radiohead*

Bonnie Raitt*

Will Ray
Hellecasters

John Raymond
Kenny G

Lou Reed

Andy Reiss*
Reba McEntire

Keith Richards
Rolling Stones

Robbie Robertson

Duke Robillard*
Fabulous Thunderbirds

Rich Robinson*
Black Crowes

Joe Rockman*
Jeff Healey

Craig Ross
Lenny Kravitz

Jeff Ross
Desert Rose Band

Mike Rutherford
Genesis, Mike + the Mechanics

Michael Joe Sagraves
Billy Ray Cyrus

Richie Sambora*
Bon Jovi

Jason Scheff*
Chicago

Keith Scott
Bryan Adams

Keith Sewell*
Ricky Skaggs

John Shanks*
Melissa Etheridge

Johnny Lee Shell*
Bonnie Raitt

Terry Shelton
Billy Ray Cyrus

Ricky Skaggs*

Skid Row*

G.E. Smith
Saturday Night Live

Betsy Smittle
Garth Brooks

Phil Solem*
The Rembrandts

Ian Spanic
Spanic Boys

Sponge*

Pops Staples*
Staple Singers

Leni Stern*

G.E. Stinson
Shadowfax

Marty Stuart

Andy Summers
The Police

Ty Tabor
King's X

Mick Taylor

Pete Townshend
The Who

The Tractors*

CELEBRITY CUSTOMER LIST

Travis Tritt

Robin Trower*

Adrian Vandenberg
Whitesnake

Jimmie Vaughan*

Stevie Ray Vaughan*

Wanda Vick*
Wild Rose

Voodoo Glow Skulls*

Waddy Wachtel

John Waite
Bad English

Jerry Jeff Walker

Joe Walsh

Steve Wariner

Brad Whitford
Aerosmith

James Wilsey
Chris Isaak

Steve Winwood

Todd Wolfe*
Sheryl Crow

Kyogi Yamamoto
Vow Wow

Dwight Yoakam

Dweezil Zappa*

The Zeros*

*Denotes Fender Endorsee

Del Breckenfeld — Director, Artist Relations

John Grunder — Custom Shop Sales Representative

Art Esparza — Senior Guitar Builder

Scott Grant — Supervisor, Custom Shop Operations

Pamalina Hovnatanian — Illustrator, Designer

George Amicay — Master Artisan, Wood Carver

Mark Duncan — Custom Shop Sales Representative

Ralph Esposito — Custom Shop Customer Relations

Jason Davis — Guitar Builder

Steve Boulanger — Custom Shop Engineer

Kenny Gin — Guitar Builder

Maria Orduno — Senior Lead Person

Dru WhiteFeather — Leather Artisan

Greg Fessler — Guitar Builder

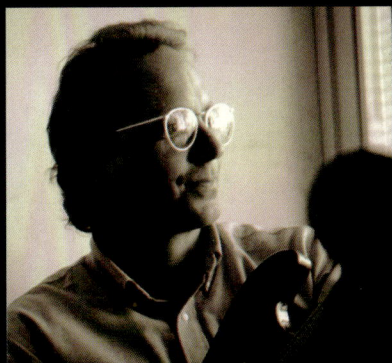

George Blanda — Research & Development,
Senior Project Engineer

Scott Buehl